Some say Bishop Richard Poore had a dream in which the Virgin Mary told him to build his new cathedral on a field called Myrifield, its present site. Others say he decided to build it where an arrow, fired from the battlements on Old Sarum, had landed. If so, it must have had a phenomenal following wind, for the distance is two miles! But for whatever reason, the position was chosen, and on 28 April 1220, Bishop Poore, his clergy and others walked there barefoot, singing the Litany.

They started digging the foundations at the east end, and at less than 4 ft they came across a deep bed of flint gravel. Provided it remains wet such gravel can support heavy weights. So they did not dig deeper: instead they built up a lime concrete base directly on the gravel, and placed the first stones at ground level. Although hardly a recipe for permanence according to the Bible, the cathedral you see today is built on sand.

In the north transept is a fine model showing the cathedral in the course of construction. Building from one end towards the other instead of from the floor upwards meant that men of all trades were kept busy, and this is clear from the model. The masons followed the foundation diggers, and were themselves followed by the glaziers, carpenters and roofers. By 1258 all the walls and roof were finished, and the Archbishop of Canterbury 'hallowed' the new building. The cathedral was considered finished in 1266.

But just think what an achievement that was. About 60,000 tons of stone had had to be mined at Chilmark, and brought by cart twelve miles to Salisbury, to be shaped and erected with only simple tools. 12,000 tons of so-called Purbeck marble, the dark, strong limestone on the pillars, came from the coast and was

moved from Poole harbour to Christchurch and the[n] up [the] Avon to Salisbury. Th[e] [roof of] the cathedral used 2,8[00 tons of] timber, and was covered with 400 tons of lead. The windows required three-quarters of an acre of glass. The effort was enormous, and when one takes into account the other building work going on, the small population, the poverty, the famines, the frequent plagues, the wars, rebellions and crusades, the achievement seems miraculous.

The cathedral is unique for its time. As it was built so quickly and on a completely new site, it is all in one style. Other medieval cathedrals were completed first by the Saxons or Normans, and

Opposite: *the Stuart royal coat of arms on the High Street Gate into the Close*
Below: *the tomb of Sir Richard Mompesson. It was originally installed on the opposite side of the choir, which is why the feet now point away from the altar*

subsequently alterations and embellishments were added in the Early English, Decorated, Perpendicular and Tudor Gothic styles, and even later periods. Standing at the west door of Salisbury Cathedral and looking the whole length of the building (something you can rarely do in cathedrals), all that you see is in the style called Early English.

There would not have been a high tower and spire then, simply low windows and a roof over the crossing. When the main cathedral was complete however, although it was not a monastic foundation, the decision was taken to add cloisters and then the incomparable Chapter House.

Finally the lantern over the crossing was dismantled, the two storeys of the tower were built up, and the spire increased to a height of 404 ft, five times the height of the ceiling over the transept. Approximately 6,400 tons of material were added, and you can see how the pillars at the corners of the crossing were bent by the weight. Remarkably, the bed of gravel under the floor held, and the spire still points above the horizon, visible for miles around.

Wandering round the interior, look out for the medieval clock on the north-west aisle. Built in 1386, it is believed to be the oldest working clock in the world. It keeps good time although constructed before the pendulum was invented, and those interested may be able to see why it ticks regularly and how it strikes the right number of strokes on the hour: there is no clock face.

Below left: *the model of the cathedral being built; it is in the north transept*
Below: *Laurence Whistler etched this prism of Steuben glass as a memorial to his brother, Rex Whistler, the artist killed in France soon after D-Day*

Right: *the view past the choir-stalls, which are mainly nineteenth century although the rear rows are thirteenth century, and past the high altar to the far window in the Trinity Chapel, which is dedicated to prisoners of conscience*

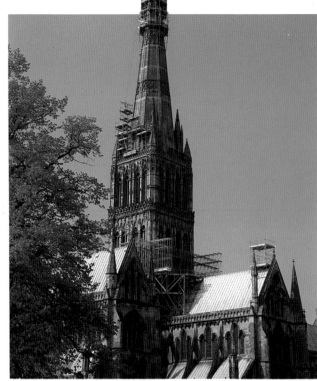

months, well worth joining unless you suffer from vertigo.

Before you go, make sure you see the cloisters, which are the largest in Britain. From them you can enter the Chapter House, when it is open. Not only is it a very beautiful building, but it contains a remarkable medieval carved frieze showing stories from the Old Testament, and a series of sculpted heads from the thirteenth century. You will also be able to see one of the four remaining copies of the Magna Carta.

In the north transept there is usually an exhibition showing what work is being done in renovating the tower and spire, and as mentioned previously, the remarkable model showing the cathedral being built is also here.

A very modern treasure can be seen in the Morning Chapel. Laurence Whistler engraved the sides of a tall glass prism in memory of his brother, the artist Rex Whistler, who was killed in World War II soon after the Normandy landing. It rotates slowly, illuminated from above, and is exquisite.

The Trinity Chapel, at the east end behind the high altar, was the first part to be completed. The rich blue east window, made by glass-makers of Chartres and erected in 1980, recalls prisoners of conscience.

Many of the tombs and monuments have interesting stories to tell, and it is best to go round with one of the guides if you have time. There are also tours of the roof area and tower during summer

Above: *the tower and spire of the cathedral will be partly surrounded with scaffolding for some years as repairs costing more than six million pounds are carried out. Prince Charles replaced the first stone in the work on the spire in September 1987.*
Below: *stonemasons carving stone to replace a pinnacle*

When Bishop Poore moved his cathedral from Old Sarum to a completely new site in 1220, it was not only the cathedral church that had to be built. His clergy needed housing, and in those days there were many of them. One in every thirty men in western Europe was a cleric. So he had a ditch dug enclosing the ecclesiastic area where they would live, and water flowed through it. He also designed the commercial part of the city outside. Everything was on a very ambitious scale, so that the Close is the largest in Britain, as the market space in the centre of the secular area used to be.

As the cathedral was commenced, the canons were allotted plots around the Close, and were told to build 'fair houses of stone' before a certain date or they would lose the sites they had been given. Each of the houses was built round a great hall, and often there was a fine undercroft. Many of the present buildings occupy the original sites, with their gardens extending down to the river, but they have been much altered and conceal their medieval beginnings behind additions of succeeding centuries. The result is a charming harmony of diverse styles and materials.

There have been some notable changes. The ditch surrounding the area was replaced with the Close wall which was begun in 1333 and used stone from Old

Below: the fourteenth-century High Street Gate into the Close is the only entrance for vehicles. A groove for a portcullis can still be seen. On the other side is a statue of King Edward VII

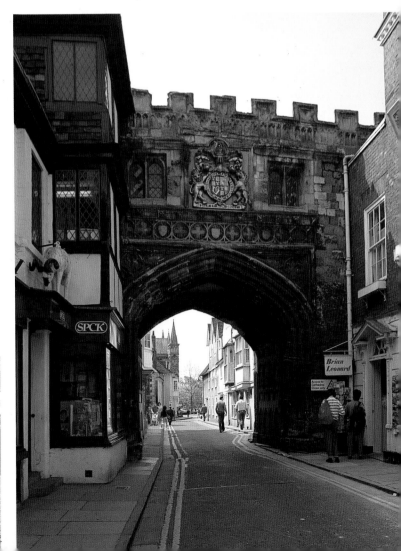

Sarum. If you walk down Exeter Street you can see many fragments of Norman carving on the surface. Four gates were incorporated. They are still locked at night. As a precaution against conflict between the ecclesiastic and secular sections of the city, the High Street Gate was fitted with a portcullis.

In the grass to the north of the cathedral a very large bell-tower stood until the eighteenth century. It was high as well as bulky, standing 200 ft tall, and was the scene of a minor skirmish during the Civil War. Around the base was an assortment of shops and alehouses, but they had mostly been removed by the end of the eighteenth century, with only the marks in the grass during a dry summer showing where the bell-tower stood.

Above: *the Bishop's Palace is now the Cathedral School. The boys eat in the thirteenth-century undercroft, but most of the building was constructed in the fifteenth, seventeenth and eighteenth centuries. The bishops lived here until 1946*

Right: *the Walton Canonry, named after Canon Isaak Walton, son of the famous angler, who lived here. Like many in the Close it is raised above a half-basement as a precaution against flood damage*

The broad areas of grass were not always so attractive. For centuries they were used for burials. In 1782 a visitor described the area thus: 'The church-yard is like a cow-common, as dirty and as neglected, and through the centre stagnates a boggy ditch.' Soon after that the area was levelled, gravestones removed and many trees planted.

The Bishop's Palace was built at the same time as the cathedral, and lies to the south-east. Except during the Commonwealth, when half of it was turned into an inn, the bishops lived in it until 1946, and these days it is the Cathedral School. The fine thirteenth-century undercroft is now the boys' dining hall.

The bishop presently lives in South Canonry, no. 71, in the south-west corner of the Close. Walking north from there you pass Leadenhall, where John Constable stayed with his friend Archbishop Fisher while painting his celebrated views of Salisbury. Next door at Walton Canonry, no. 69, Isaak Walton, the author of *The Compleat Angler,* used to stay with his son, and the neighbouring house, Myles Place, no. 68, was the home of Arthur Bryant the historian.

The King's House earned its name when King James I was entertained there. Much of the central section is fifteenth century. Now it contains the Salisbury and South Wiltshire Museum which will be described in detail later. Beyond it you will pass houses which formed part of the Sarum St Michael teacher training college, and then, passing North Canonry, no. 60,

Left: *the coat of arms high on the College of Matrons*
Below: *the College of Matrons was built for £793 12s 8d in 1682/3 with twenty rooms on each side and eight oak staircases*

Top: *Arundells, the 1749 house where Mr Edward Heath lives*
Centre: *the Theological College stands where Bishop Richard Poore founded the Cathedral School of Theology when the cathedral was built. The main building is seventeenth-century but the chapel was built in 1881*

you can see Arundells standing well back behind the railings. This is the home of Mr Edward Heath.

The Wardrobe, no. 58, started in 1258 as the Bishop's Storehouse, but little remains of the original building. It houses the headquarters and museum of the Duke of Edinburgh's Regiment. Beyond is a series of old houses to the end of the row, and not far round the corner you reach Mompesson House, no. 53, a

magnificent eighteenth-century house belonging to the National Trust, which is described in more detail later.

The North, or High Street, Gate dates from the fourteenth and fifteenth centuries, and is the main entrance for vehicles. Its small size means large removal lorries cannot get into the Close. The gate is more impressive from the outside.

Not far inside the gate, on the east side, is the College of Matrons, nos. 39 to 46. Instituted by Bishop Seth Ward, it may have been designed by his friend Sir Christopher Wren. Widows and unmarried daughters of clergy in the diocese live here. The Bishop may have built it originally for a former sweetheart whose clergyman husband had died.

Walking along the north edge of the Close, 'Aula le Stage' is a thirteenth-century house rebuilt in 1540. In the fifteenth century the house had a small tower and was the only building in the Close with a third storey or 'stage', hence its name.

Further along, the Theological College, no. 19, stands where the Cathedral School of Theology was founded when the new cathedral was built. Much of the present building dates from the seventeenth century. Opposite, Bishop's Walk leads past the Deanery, the office of the Dean and Chapter and the Organist's House, but if you walk straight on you reach St Ann's Gate with Malmesbury House beside it. The top part of the gate, now an architects' office, was a chapel, and Handel is reputed to have given his first concert in England here.

Left: *Bishop's Walk, with Georgian additions to Cromwellian houses, is where the Dean lives. It also contains the offices of the Dean and Chapter*

Three houses in the Close should be visited if possible: Malmesbury House, Mompesson House, and the Museum in the King's House.

Malmesbury House

This fine house beside St Ann's Gate has a striking sundial on its side, with 'Life's but a walking shadow' painted on it. Passing visitors photograph it over the wall, but the house is open to the public at various times and worth exploring.

Some of it originates from 1399 when it was extensively rebuilt, but most of the older section dates from further alterations in 1660. The Harris family, who were tenants of the house from 1660 to 1870, at an annual rent of 27s 4d (£1.37) throughout that time, knew many illustrious people. Among their guests were writers like James Boswell and

Left: just inside St Ann's Gate into the Close, this sundial can be seen on the wall of Malmesbury House

Below: Malmesbury House was enlarged in the seventeenth and eighteenth centuries on the site of some small medieval houses

LIFE'S BUT A WALKING SHADOW

1749

THIS IS LIFE ETERNAL THAT THEY MAY KNOW THEE THE ONLY TRUE GOD, AND JESUS CHRIST, WHOM THOU HAST SENT.
ST JOHN. CHAPTER 17. VERSE 3.

Above: *the library at Malmesbury House is a fine example of 'Strawberry Hill' Gothic*

Right: *the 32-foot-high entrance hall and staircase, with fine plasterwork and a chandelier from Versailles. The present owner had to replace the rotten wooden floor with a stone floor during extensive renovations, and he decorated the walls and ceiling in a style reminiscent of Wedgwood pottery*

Opposite, top: *five of the 370 glasses dating from about 1770 in a collection in Mompesson House*

Opposite, bottom: *built in 1680 and improved in 1701, Mompesson House now belongs to the National Trust, which has furnished it to reflect the grace of eighteenth-century living*

Dr Samuel Johnson ('Awkward, beastly in his person,' according to Mrs Harris, 'he eats quantities most unthankfully!') and Edward Gibbon the historian. Artists included Sir Joshua Reynolds, and the composer George Frederic Handel was a frequent visitor.

Downstairs you can see round the Drawing Room, the Dining Room and the Hall, as well as the Music Room in the new addition at the back of the house. Upstairs, in the older section with its narrow passages and massive walls, is the Charles II room, where the King is said to have hidden in a cubby hole during his escape to the Continent after the Battle of Worcester. After his restoration the King visited again in 1665 when the Great Plague was widespread in London.

Mompesson House

Charles Mompesson built this house in 1701, and his brother-in-law embellished it with plaster-work ceilings and other additions so that what remains is a fine example of eighteenth-century style. This is reflected in the furniture and fittings placed here by the National Trust. Wandering through the rooms and lobbies

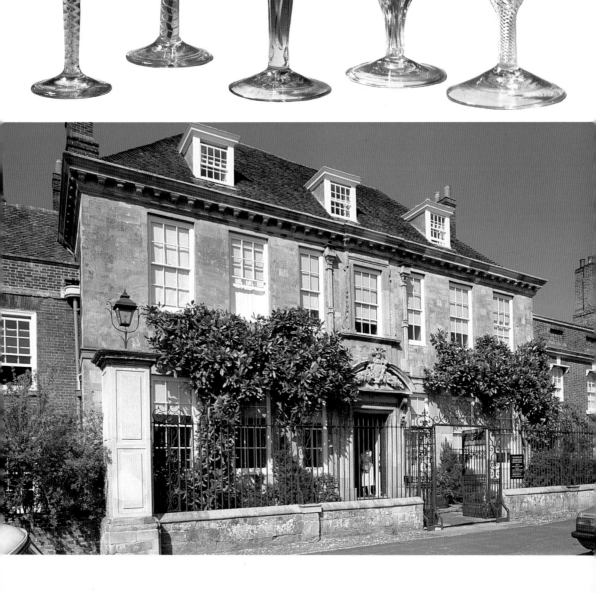

Below: *the drawing room at Mompesson House. The house has been used by judges at the local assize court, and from 1947 to 1951 by the Bishop* gives a delightful sense of gracious living during that elegant age. The garden is beautiful too.

Against this background is evidence of the families who have lived here, especially Barbara Townsend, many of whose paintings are on view. She was a remarkable woman and a real character who lived in the house for her whole life, almost ninety-seven years. There is also an impressive collection of more than 340 eighteenth-century drinking glasses.

The King's House

The Abbot of Sherborne built this house in the thirteenth century, and it was used by his successors until the Reformation. It is believed that King Richard III was staying here when he ordered the execution of the Duke of Buckingham, who had been his staunch supporter and then rebelled against him, in the courtyard of the Blue Boar inn beside the market square. The duke's head was brought to the king here, it is said, and stains on the floorboards in one of the rooms, which can never be removed, are believed to have been his blood.

King James I stayed here more than once, hence the name. But in the eighteenth century it was too big for one family to live in, and was split up, part of it housing the beginnings of the teacher training college, later the College of Sarum St Michael.

Now it houses the Salisbury and South Wiltshire Museum – one of the best in the country. The museum started as a collection of objects found in the old channels along the streets when the sewers were constructed. When the city was founded, the streets had 'little streamlets and arms derived out of the Avon' flowing along them. But they were not kept clean, and rubbish and sewage were discharged into them, so that they spread disease rather than prevented it. In the early nineteenth century they were covered up, deep sewers were constructed and a piped water supply was brought in. When the ditches were dug out, a remarkable collection of historic objects was found, and almost 14,000 were saved. They became the nucleus of the museum.

Apart from the section on the history of Salisbury, including St Christopher the Salisbury Giant, his attendant hobby-horse Hobnob, and many other historical items, the museum's galleries cover Stonehenge and prehistory in Wiltshire, as well as containing ceramics, costume, pottery and other features of the permanent and temporary displays.

Below: *almost opposite the west end of the cathedral, the King's House is so called because King James I stayed here. It now houses the Salisbury and South Wiltshire Museum*

The market place is the centre of the commercial part of the city, and is very large. Yet when Bishop Poore laid it out in 1220 it was far larger. Streets like Fish Row and Butcher Row, Ox Row and Oatmeal Row, alleyways running between the market stalls, were parts of it. But in time stallholders erected permanent shelters to cover their wares, filled in the sides to make shops, and then built upper storeys to live in.

Street names reveal where various goods were sold, and the Poultry Cross is the only remaining one of four original crosses which focused the sale of poultry,

Main picture: *the fifteenth-century Poultry Cross is the only survivor of the original four crosses which marked where sales of poultry, milk, cheese, livestock and wool were centred*

Inset, top left: *markets have been held on every Tuesday and Saturday since 1361*

Inset, bottom left: *the Guildhall, built in 1795 to replace the Elizabethan Council House which was destroyed by fire*

Inset, right: *the Jacobean Joiners' Hall in St Ann's Street*

cheese, wool and cattle.

The city charter of 1227 instituted a weekly market in the space, but with its success it was held more frequently, almost daily, until complaints of unfair competition were received from Wilton and Old Sarum. Markets were limited to Tuesdays and Saturdays in 1361, which is when they have been held ever since.

In one corner of the market place stands the Guildhall, built in 1795. Many of the other buildings surrounding the space are far older, and form a delightful, compatible mixture of ages and styles. The same is true for the

Top: *the King's Arms Hotel in Exeter Street has changed little since supporters of Charles II used it to plan his escape after the Battle of Worcester, signalling by lamp to Malmesbury House opposite*

Above: *part of the new Maltings shopping development. This may be the site where the Bishop of Salisbury owned a mill in 1086. In the nineteenth century there were ten malthouses here*

place. Stroll down Catherine Street and St John Street, visiting the King's Arms Hotel if you like old buildings and time permits, and turn into St Ann Street. At the far end you will find the Joiners' Hall, where the carved wooden corbels below the first floor windows are said to be caricatures of the city councillors and feature figures with both male and female characteristics. The view from there, with the cathedral spire topping the varied house fronts and St Ann's Gate, is perhaps the loveliest street scene in the city.

Your walk back to the market place can be by Love Lane, the surrounding streets, and the even, small scale of the buildings is a relic of the city's foundation. The domestic and commercial area was divided into blocks called 'chequers', not quite symmetrical as water channels had to run along them. The plots for tenements in these chequers were approximately 35 m by 15 m, rented out at about 12d (5p) a year.

Most of the shop fronts are clearly modern, but look up and the top sections are generally much older. Upstairs in Watson's china shop in Queen Street opposite the Guildhall, for example, you can see the ancient beams, medieval windows and old panelling.

The most interesting streets are south and east of the market medieval 'red light' district, and Trinity Street. On the north side of this walk into Trinity Hospital, founded as an act of penance in 1379 by Agnes of Bottenham, an ex-innkeeper and brothel owner. It was entirely rebuilt in 1792, and the chapel across the courtyard is worth seeing.

Walk along Ivy Street and New Street and you reach the High Street, with Mitre Corner the house on your left. Said to be the site of the first house built outside the Close, this is where each new bishop is robed before being led in through High Street Gate by the Dean and Chapter. Crane Street

opposite is also worth exploring, and you can turn right to amble along the riverside, cross Bridge Street and walk over a bridge by the Bishop's Mill to enter the new Maltings shopping development.

Then, if you want a break from buildings before visiting St Thomas's Church or some of the inns, walk over to the Queen Elizabeth Gardens in the south west, or the bigger Churchill Gardens in the south east. Here are riverside walks of singular peace and charm, always with the marvellous background of the cathedral's incomparable tower and spire.

Below: *St Ann's Gate was built at the same time as the Close wall in the 1330s. In the room over the gate Handel is believed to have given his first concert in England*

St Thomas's Church

Before the masons started to build the new cathedral, a wooden chapel was built for them to worship in. That was the beginning of St Thomas's Church, dedicated to St Thomas à Becket, which lies a short distance west of the market place. Stone soon replaced the timber, chapels were added on the north side and a separate bell-tower on the south started in 1400. More additions were made, including the side chapel which joined the bell-tower to the church, and the whole in harmony, so that today the impression is of a particularly light, pleasant and mainly Perpendicular style church.

The principal feature striking visitors is the picture round the chancel arch. It is the largest Doom painting in the world. In the 1470s when it was painted, congregations could not read and the services were in Latin, so that the walls of every church were painted with pictures impressing on the memories of the people the main stories of the Christian faith. The Doom, or last judgement of Christ, was the most popular subject, and smaller, less well preserved versions still exist in a hundred or more churches.

High up in the centre the figure of Christ sits on a rainbow, the buildings of New Jerusalem on each side. The Virgin and presumably St Joseph kneel beside him and angels nearby hold the instruments of his passion: the spear and sponge, and the pillar against which he was scourged. The crown of thorns hangs on the Cross, which is T-shaped. Below, in a row, sit the twelve disciples.

The message of the painting lies down the two sides. On the left, emerging from their tombs, some still in their shrouds of wool, are the blessed, and they are conducted up to the New Jerusalem where the inhabitants watch from windows and parapets. The right side is the frightening one. Here the damned, including crowned heads and at least one bishop, are conducted into the giant red dragon and the sea of fire as described in Revelation.

At the time of the Reformation the painting was whitewashed, and it was not until the end of the last century that it was finally uncovered and left revealed for all to see.

This is not the only old painting in the church. On the wall of the Lady Chapel you can see representations of the Annunciation, Visitation and Nativity, which are even older.

On the walls of the church are fine hatchments, and there are other items of interest, including two old mace stands. The wooden ceilings have many carved angels, and the organ, which was

Below: St Thomas's Church is on the site of the wooden chapel built for the cathedral masons, possibly the first building of New Sarum. The square bell-tower was built separately in 1400, and joined to the church when the south aisle was constructed about 150 years later

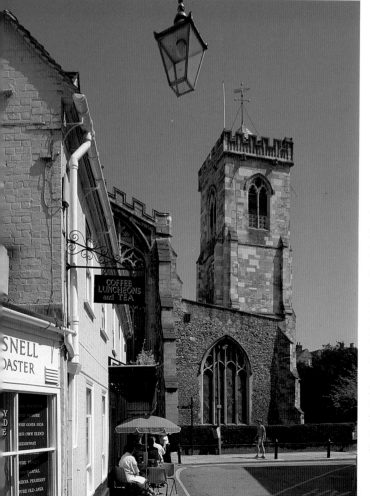

presented to the cathedral in 1792 by King George III, was transferred to St Thomas's in 1877 when the cathedral installed a larger one.

In the bell-tower outside, two quarterjacks, installed in 1582, strike the quarters. Carved in mail with open helmets and fine faces, they would have been obvious when the market place extended to St Thomas's, but to see them now it is best to enter the church-yard through a small passage from Minster Street.

Above: *the interior of St Thomas's Church, showing the magnificent Doom painting*

Inns and Alehouses

For centuries the local hostelry or inn has played an important part in the lives of ordinary citizens. Besides being places to buy drinks, they have provided entertainment, libraries, education and centres for political and guild activities.

There are some fine historical pubs in Salisbury worth visiting, and the following will give a taste of the variety.

Unfortunately the most important of the old inns, the Old George in the High Street, is no more, but parts of it can be seen in the Bay Tree restaurant. The room with the gables, over the entrance to the Old George shopping mall, should be seen if possible. Cromwell slept here on 17 October 1645, and Samuel Pepys on 11 June 1668 enjoyed 'a silk bed and a very good diet, but next day, on paying the reckoning, it was so exorbitant I was mad.'

The Haunch of Venison in Minster Street is full of character and dates from the fourteenth century. Just inside the door on the right is one of the smallest bars in the country, while in the room up a few stairs, you will find on the left of the fireplace

a severed hand holding some eighteenth-century playing cards. Perhaps a relic of rough justice for cheating!

The Pheasant in Salt Lane was the centre for the shoemakers, and the old Shoemakers' Guild Hall is incorporated in the building.

In medieval times the Red Lion housed craftsmen building the cathedral. The courtyard has a 150-year-old creeper, which hangs like a curtain over the entrance and is most remarkable when it turns a deep red and has the midday sun shining behind it. This was the terminus for the Old Original Salisbury Flying Machine, a coach hung on steel springs, which ran a daily service to and from Ludgate Hill in London.

Milford Street and Ivy Street have further examples of interesting pubs. No longer brewing their own ales, they attract people these days by offering very good bar snacks as well as drink.

Below: *The Pheasant Inn, Salt Lane, was known as The Crispin in the fifteenth century, and it was the centre for the shoemakers. The old Shoemakers' Guild Hall is incorporated in the building*

Theatre

In Tudor times actors performed Shakespeare's plays at Wilton House, and it is known that at least one pub staged plays in the eighteenth century. The first purpose-built theatre in the city was probably the New Theatre in 1777, and others followed. Since then theatres have had bad times as well as good, but the present Salisbury Playhouse, opened in 1976 by Sir Alec Guinness, is thriving. The volume of its production output far exceeds that of any regional theatre of comparable size. Audiences are attracted from all over Wiltshire, Hampshire and Dorset, and performances are often sold out, so you are advised to book early. Almost every year recently it has held the record for the highest box office attendances of any regional theatre.

Cinema

In contrast with the theatre, the Odeon cinema in New Canal is not in a new building, in fact part of it is very old indeed. Inside the doors you pass into a medieval hall which formed part of the house of a celebrated character, four times mayor, called John Halle. The cinema itself has been divided into three screens.

Arts Centre

Salisbury Arts Centre also has an old home, and is to be found in St Edmund's Church in Bedwin Street. When the parish was merged with St Thomas's Church and the building was redundant, a group of volunteers began using it for various arts and activities, and in time this was put on a sound footing and was granted financial support. Now it offers a wide range of events, workshops and activities and also has a small restaurant.

Racecourse

In March 1584 'there was a race run with horses, at the farthest three miles from Sarum . . . and the Earl of Cumberland won the golden bell, which was valued at £50 and better.' The Earl later fought against the Spanish Armada.

The same site has been used for Salisbury Races from that time, and meetings have been held regularly since 1722.

Sports

The municipal swimming pool is in College Street, not far from the city centre. The building also contains a health and fitness centre with sun-beds, sauna, spa bath and multi-gym.

There are two golf courses nearby, Salisbury and South Wilts course at Netherhampton, and High Post club on the Amesbury road. Tennis courts can be found in Victoria Park. The council intends to build a large new leisure centre on Butts Field within the next few years, a little way from the city centre.

Below: *the fifteenth-century banqueting hall of the merchant John Halle forms the remarkable foyer of the Odeon cinema (photo courtesy the Salisbury Journal)*

STONEHENGE AND AVEBURY

Wiltshire is by far the richest county in Britain for pre-historic remains, and many people come to Salisbury simply because of its proximity to Stonehenge. Yet all over Salisbury Plain long barrows, round barrows, earthworks and ditches can be found. What is the reason?

In 4000 BC what is now broad plain was probably dense woodland. Then settlers came from Europe, bringing seed corn and domesticated animals. They began to clear the forests, till the soil until it was exhausted, and then move on to fell more forest. By 3000 BC the area probably resembled today's landscape.

The more efficient farming and storage of food supported the population easily, and there was labour to spare for communal operations. One of the results was Stonehenge, which lies about ten miles north of Salisbury.

Stonehenge

Stonehenge is unique: there is nothing like it anywhere else in the world. Its exact purpose is unknown, but its alignments, for instance with the rising sun at the summer solstice, cannot be accidental, so it probably had astronomical as well as religious purposes.

Construction began in about 3000 BC, the bluestones coming 240 miles by raft, boat, sledges and rollers from the Preseli mountains in south-west Wales. But the main sarsen stones were erected about a thousand years later, around 2000 BC, when Abraham was leaving Ur of the Chaldees and a thousand years before Solomon and David lived. Yet this was a task which needed a remarkable degree of social organisation. Transport of the eighty sarsen stones from north Wiltshire would have taken about a thousand men working together several years. Remember that when you see the immense stones.

Unfortunately, such is the number of visitors each summer they cannot get close to the stones but are kept beyond some ropes a little way away. Going round, signs explain the stages of development of the monument. However, a fuller and more exciting explanation and exhibition can be found in the Stonehenge Gallery in the Salisbury Museum in the Close.

Avebury

Less than twenty miles north of Stonehenge is an older, less visited and in some ways more impressive monument, Avebury. The village intrudes into the ancient circle of stones, and many of the walls of the buildings contain broken pieces of stones missing from the ring. The ditches and ring are much bigger than Stonehenge, and you can wander among them and touch the remaining megaliths of the ring.

From it stretches a long stone avenue, and there are walks to Silbury Hill, the tallest mystery in ancient Europe. Carbon dating has shown that this mound, more than 40 m high, was begun in approximately 2750 BC. It was constructed from tightly rammed chalk.

Another attraction nearby is the West Kennet Long Barrow. You can enter the sarsen-lined burial chamber that occupies about one-sixth of the mound's length. As you go round it reflect that the first bodies were buried in it 5,000 years ago.

Finally, visit the museum, the church and other attractions of the village.

Right: *the main prehistoric ring of stones at Avebury. Dating back to about 2600 BC, it consisted of almost 100 unshaped sarsen stones about three to four metres high, arranged in a circle of 350 metres diameter. From it for a mile and a half ran the West Kennet avenue of stones*

Left: *Silbury Hill is the tallest artefact in prehistoric Europe, but the reason for its construction is unknown. The Romans used it as a marker when making their roads in the area*

S alisbury is an excellent centre for the tourist, within easy reach of stately homes, gardens, the New Forest, the coast, and other places of interest.

Right: *Wilton House*

Wilton

Three miles west of Salisbury is the pleasant little town of Wilton. Once much bigger than Old Sarum, indeed the county town of Wiltshire or Wiltonshire, the royal palace of King Egbert and the abbey founded by King Alfred were built here.

But as New Sarum grew, Wilton diminished. The royal palace disappeared – the Georgian houses of Kingsbury Square probably cover it – and the abbey, which was rich and powerful for 600 years, ended with the dissolution of the monasteries.

The abbey and lands were given by King Henry VIII to William Herbert, first Earl of Pembroke, and they have remained in the family ever since. William Herbert pulled down the abbey and built a fine house which his descendants enlarged and embellished. They were men of great wealth and taste, and Wilton House is one of the stately houses of Britain, with a

remarkable collection of paintings and sculpture. Kings and queens have been entertained, and many illustrious people have stayed and worked here. During World War II the magnificent Double Cube room was the Southern Command headquarters and the operations room for Eisenhower and Montgomery when D-Day was planned.

In addition to the house, there are extensive and beautiful grounds, an adventure play-ground, a computer-controlled model train network, a collection of 7,000 miniature soldiers, and the Pembroke Palace Doll's House, among other attractions.

Wilton itself is an attractive small town with a traditional market on Thursdays. The parish church is an Italianate basilica, and the Wilton Royal Carpet Factory makes some of the world's finest carpets.

Left: Broadlands, Lord Mountbatten's home in Romsey

Romsey

Broadlands, a fine Palladian house which belonged to Lord Mountbatten, is at Romsey, fourteen miles south east of Salisbury. Apart from the fine furniture, rooms and grounds, the exhibition of Lord Mountbatten's life and career is worth seeing. While in Romsey, visit Romsey Abbey and King John's House.

Breamore

About eight miles south of Salisbury beside the A338 to Ringwood, Breamore (pronounced Bremmer) House can be seen across fields on the right, and should not be missed. Hardly changed in the last 400 years, the Great Hall, dining-room, drawing-rooms and bedrooms have beautiful proportions and contain fine furniture and many works of art. The kitchen has a collection of coppers, a beer-wagon, and many old cooking instruments.

In the outbuildings are a carriage museum and an extensive countryside museum. From beside the hall a walk starts up through the woods to an ancient miz-maze.

Breamore church was built in 980 AD and its Saxon origins can be clearly seen from the tower, the arch into the transept, seven double-splayed windows and the rood in the porch. A remarkable Anglo-Saxon inscription curves round the south arch inside the tower.

Above: Romsey Abbey

Above: *the New
Forest*

The New Forest

The 146 square miles of the New
Forest start ten miles south of
Salisbury. William the Conqueror
created it in 1079 by reserving the
whole area for hunting. Whole
villages were moved, and the
peasants were forbidden to
enclose their land or clear trees.
In compensation they were
awarded rights, which still exist,
for grazing domestic animals.
The ponies and cattle to be seen
wandering round have their
owners' brands on them. Visitors
must not feed them.

Trees are there in abundance –
the area provided the oaks for
Nelson's and other ships – but
much of the New Forest is open
space. It is the only such large,